Mediterranean Diet Meal Prep

Easy and Healthy Mediterranean Diet Recipes to Prep, Grab and Go. 21-Day Fix Meal Plan to Lose Weight as Fast as Possible

Brandon Hearn © 2019

Table of Contents

Introduction

The Mediterranean diet is centuries older than the nutritional research that is behind it. It's an approach to eating where you can enjoy pasta, whole grains, in season fruits, crisp and roasted vegetables and even breads. You can have creamy yogurt, seafood, cheeses, spices, meat and even the occasional glass of wine.

This diet includes a pattern of food choices that came from the countries that surround the Mediterranean Sea. These countries include Lebanon, Egypt, Algeria, Israel, Turkey, Morocco, Greek, Spain, Italy, Southern France, Libya and even Tunisia. You'll find that each country offers a new array of cuisine that you can chow down and enjoy, meaning this book is just a glimpse of what the Mediterranean diet has to offer you.

There are many health benefits associated with the Mediterranean diet, including reductions in blood pressure, weight and even blood lipids. It can help to reduce your blood sugar levels long term and it can also lessen your chance of dealing with a chronic disease.

As we age our brains shrink which contribute to Alzheimer's, but this diet will help you to maintain your brain size. This can help to lower your risk of Alzheimer's in the future. It can also help with dementia. Arthritis can also be helped with the Mediterranean diet because it can help the pain that results from rheumatoid and osteoarthritis. Asthma can eve ben helped because it can help protect against the effects of asthma, especially in children! You can say goodbye to cardiovascular disease since this diet has many heart healthy benefits. Diabetes is also helped since blood sugar is controlled much more easily. High blood pressure and high cholesterol because this diet will help to lower "bad cholesterol" such as your LDL levels. As you can see, there is various reasons why the Mediterranean diet will help you to achieve your health goals. The best part is that if you know what to look for, then it's easy to find Mediterranean food on almost an menu. Just try to be careful of your sodium intake when eating out. Luckily, with this twenty-one day meal plan you'll get started on the right track!

21 Day Meal Plan

You'll find every recipe in this meal plan in the book. With this twenty-one day meal plan, you'll be able to adjust to the Mediterranean diet without needing to buy ingredients that are hard to find or purchase. You can even use recipes creatively. You'll find that some breakfast recipes make healthy desserts, for example, or some dinner leftovers can double as lunches later in the week.

Day 1

Breakfast: Ricotta & Pear Bake
Lunch: Eggplant Rolls
Dinner: Vegetable Stew
Dessert: Honey Almonds

Day 2

Breakfast: Banana Bowl
Lunch: Pesto Pasta
Dinner: Easy Greek Soup
Dessert: Yogurt Cake with Figs

Day 3

Breakfast: Lentil Omelet
Lunch: Lemon Faro Bowl
Dinner: Roasted Squash Bisque
Dessert: Nutty Honey Baked Pears

Day 4

Breakfast: Poached Pears
Lunch: Grilled Fish with Lemons
Dinner: Chicken & Asparagus
Dessert: Yogurt Cake with Figs

Day 5

Breakfast: Cappuccino Muffins
Lunch: Pistachio Arugula Salad
Dinner: Seafood Gumbo
Dessert: Glazed Apples

Day 6

Breakfast: Marinated Berries
Lunch: Lebanese Delight
Dinner: Easy Stuffed Peppers
Dessert: Vanilla Yogurt Affogato

Day 7

Breakfast: Easy Apricot Biscotti
Lunch: Tomato Tabbouleh
Dinner: Chicken & Asparagus
Dessert: Dark Chocolate Strawberries

Day 8

Breakfast: Lentil Omelet
Lunch: Lemon Faro Bowl
Dinner: Red Onion Tilapia + Raisin Rice Pilaf
Dessert: Vermicelli Pudding

Day 9

Breakfast: Fruit Bulgur
Lunch: Pesto Walnut Noodles
Dinner: Easy Stuffed Peppers
Dessert: Quinoa Bars

Day 10

Breakfast: Goat Cheese & Pepper Eggs
Lunch: Mediterranean Quiche
Dinner: Vegetable Stew
Dessert: Marinated Berries

Day 11

Breakfast: Apple Quinoa Bowl
Lunch: Heavenly Quinoa
Dinner: Chickpea Patties + Flavorful Braised Kale
Dessert: Roasted Plum with Almonds

Day 12

Breakfast: Watermelon Bowl
Lunch: Chickpea & Red Pepper Delight
Dinner: Seafood Gumbo
Dessert: Glazed Apples

Day 13

Breakfast: Quinoa Bars
Lunch: Heavenly Quinoa
Dinner: Roasted Squash Bisque
Dessert: Chocolate Fruit Kebabs

Day 14

Breakfast: Mediterranean Toast
Lunch: Pesto Pasta
Dinner: Easy Greek Soup
Dessert: Honey Almonds

Day 15

Breakfast: Goat Cheese & Pepper Eggs
Lunch: Bean Salad
Dinner: Beef Kofta + Mediterranean Sweet Potato
Dessert: Stone Fruit with Whipped Ricotta

Day 16

Breakfast: Watermelon Bowl
Lunch: Tomato Tabbouleh
Dinner: Red Onion Tilapia + Basil Tomato Skewers
Dessert: Cappuccino Muffins

Day 17

Breakfast: Banana Bowl
Lunch: Red Bean & Green Salad
Dinner: Chickpea Patties + Potato Salad
Dessert: Watermelon Bowl

Day 18

Breakfast: Red Egg Skillet
Lunch: Chickpea Salad
Dinner: Chicken & Asparagus
Dessert: Honey Almonds

Day 19

Breakfast: Mediterranean Toast
Lunch: Eggplant Rolls
Dinner: Red Onion Tilapia + Pesto Walnut Noodles
Dessert: Chocolate Fruit Kebabs

Day 20

Breakfast: Lentil Omelet
Lunch: Pistachio Arugula Salad
Dinner: Beef Kofta + Olives with Feta
Dessert: Stone Fruit with Whipped Ricotta

Day 21

Breakfast: Baked Apple Delight
Lunch: Chickpea Salad
Dinner: Herby Chicken with Potatoes
Dessert: Poached Pears

Breakfast Recipes

Ricotta & Pear Bake

Serves: 4

Time: 25 Minutes

Calories: 312

Protein: 17 Grams

Fat: 17 Grams

Carbs: 23 Grams

Sodium: 130 mg

Ingredients:

- 16 Ounce Whole Milk Ricotta Cheese
- 2 Eggs, Large
- 1 Tablespoon Sugar
- ¼ Cup Whole Wheat Flour
- 1 Teaspoon Vanilla Extract, Pure
- ¼ Teaspoon Nutmeg
- 2 Tablespoon Water
- 1 Pear, Cored & Diced
- 1 Tablespoon Honey, Raw

Directions:

1. Start by heating your oven to 400, and then get out four ramekins that are six ounces each. Grease them with cooking spray.

2. Get out a bowl and beat your eggs, flour, sugar, ricotta, vanilla, and nutmeg together. Spoon this mixture into your ramekins, baking for about twenty-five minutes. The ricotta should be almost set.

3. Remove it from the oven, and allow it to cool.

4. While you bake your ricotta get out a saucepan and place it over medium heat. Simmer your pears in water for ten minutes. They should soften, and then remove them from heat. Stir your honey in, and then serve the ricotta ramekins topped with your cooked pears.

Fruit Bulgur

Serves: 5

Time: 15 Minutes

Calories: 301

Protein: 9 Grams

Fat: 6 Grams

Carbs: 57 Grams

Sodium: 40 mg

Ingredients:

- 2 Cups Milk, 2%
- 1 ½ Cups Bulgur, Uncooked
- ½ Teaspoon Cinnamon
- 2 Cups Dark Sweet cherries, Frozen
- 8 Figs, Dried & Chopped
- ½ Cup Almonds, Chopped
- ¼ Cup Mint, Fresh & Chopped
- ½ Cup Almonds, Chopped
- Warm 2% Milk to Serve

Directions:

1. Get out a medium saucepan and combine your water, cinnamon, bulgur and milk together. Stir it once and bring it just to a boil. Once it begins to boil then cover it, and then reduce your heat to medium-low. Allow it to simmer for ten minutes. The liquid should be absorbed.

2. Turn the heat off, but keep your pan on the stove. Stir in your frozen cherries. You don't need to thaw them, and then ad din your almonds and figs. Stir well before covering for a minute.

3. Stir your mint in, and then serve with warm milk drizzled over it.

Goat Cheese & Pepper Eggs

Serves: 5

Time: 10 Minutes

Calories: 201

Protein: 15 Grams

Fat: 15 Grams

Carbs: 5 Grams

Sodium: 166 mg

Ingredients:

- 1 Cup Bell Pepper, Chopped
- 1 ½ Teaspoons Olive Oil
- 2 Cloves Garlic, Minced
- 6 Eggs, Large
- ¼ Teaspoon Sea Salt, Fine
- 2 Tablespoons Water
- ½ Cup Goat Cheese, Crumbled

- 2 Tablespoons Mint, fresh & Chopped

Directions:

1. Start by getting a large skillet out and placing it over medium-high heat. Add in your oil. Once your oil begins to shimmer add in your peppers and allow them to cook for five minutes. Stir occasionally, and then add in your garlic and cook a minute more.

2. While your peppers cook whisk your slat, water and eggs together. Turn the heat to medium-low. Pour your egg mixture over the peppers, and then let them cook for about two minutes without stirring them. They should set on the bottom before you sprinkle your goat cheese over top.

3. Cook your eggs for another two minutes, and then serve with fresh mint.

Lentil Omelet

Serves: 2

Time: 15 Minutes

Calories: 242

Protein: 19 Grams

Fat: 9 Grams

Carbs: 22 Grams

Sodium: 129 mg

Ingredients:

- 8 Avocado Slices for Garnish
- ½ Cup Grape Tomatoes, Chopped for Garnish
- ½ Cup Lentils, Canned, Drained & Rinsed
- 1 Cup Asparagus, Chopped
- ¼ Cup Onion, Chopped
- 1 Tablespoon Thyme
- 4 Eggs, Whisked

Directions:

1. Get out a bowl and whisk you egg and thyme together. Place it to the side.
2. Heat a skillet using medium heat, and cook your onion and asparagus for two to three minutes. Add in your lentils, cooking for another two minutes. It should be heated all the way through. Reduce the heat to low.

3. Get out a skillet and place it over medium heat, whisking your eggs again before adding them to the skillet. Cook for two to three minutes. They should be set on the bottom.

4. Spread your lentil and asparagus mixture on one half. Cook for another two minutes before folding the egg over the lentil filling. Cook for another two minutes.

5. Repeat with your remaining ingredients to create a second omelet.

6. Garnish with avocado before serving.

Apple Quinoa Bowl

Serves: 2

Time: 25 Minutes

Calories: 360

Protein: 14 Grams

Fat: 13 Grams

Carbs: 49 Grams

Sodium: 151 mg

Ingredients:

- ½ Cup Quinoa, Uncooked
- 1 Cup Vanilla Almond Milk, Unsweetened
- ½ Teaspoon Cinnamon
- 2 Cinnamon Sticks
- Pinch Sea Salt

Toppings:

- 2 Tablespoons Almonds, Sliced
- 2 Tablespoons Hemp Seeds
- 1 Cup Apple, Chopped
- Honey to Sweeten

Directions:

1. Rinse your quinoa using a colander and make sure it's well drained. Transfer it to a saucepan with your cinnamon, cinnamon sticks, almond milk and salt. Bring it to a simmer, and cover. Reduce the heat to low, allowing it to simmer for fifteen minutes.

2. Remove it from heat and then let it rest for five minutes. Your almond milk should be absorbed, and your quinoa should be cooked all the way through.

3. Divide between bowls and top with your toppings.

Overnight Chia Pudding

Serves: 2

Time: 8 Hours 5 Minutes

Calories: 732

Protein: 13 Grams

Fat: 63 Grams

Carbs: 41 Grams

Sodium: 38 mg

Ingredients:

- ½ Cup Chia Seeds
- 2n Cups Coconut Milk, Light
- 3 Teaspoons Honey, Divided
- ¼ Cup Banana, Sliced
- ¼ Cup Raspberries, Fresh
- ½ Tablespoon Almonds, Sliced
- ½ Tablespoon Walnuts, Chopped
- 2 Teaspoons Cocoa Powder, Unsweetened & Divided

Directions:

1. Mix your chia seeds, coconut milk, and two teaspoons of honey together in a bowl. Portion it out into mason jars, and refrigerate for eight hours or overnight.
2. Remove them from the fridge, and top with raspberries, almonds, banana, cocoa and walnuts. Drizzle with remaining honey.

Banana Bowl

Serves: 4

Time: 10 Minutes

Calories: 440

Protein: 14.5 Grams

Fat: 16.6 Grams

Carbs: 49.2 Grams

Sodium: 73 mg

Ingredients:

- 4 Cups Greek Yogurt, Vanilla
- 2 Bananas, Sliced
- ¼ Cup Flax Seed Meal
- ¼ cup Peanut Butter, Creamy & Natural
- 1 Teaspoon Nutmeg

Directions:

1. Divide your yogurt between four bowl and top with bananas.
2. Get out a microwave safe bowl and melt your butter in ten second intervals. Drizzle it over your banana slices, and garnish with flax seed and nutmeg before serving.

Quinoa Bars

Serves: 6

Time: 10 Minutes

Calories: 110

Protein: 4.7 Grams

Fat: 1.9 Grams

Carbs: 45.9 Grams

Sodium: 59 mg

Ingredients:

- 4 Semi Sweet Chocolate Bars, 4 Ounces Each & Chopped
- ½ Teaspoon Vanilla Extract, Pure
- 1 Tablespoon Peanut Butter
- 1 Cup Quinoa, Dry

Directions:

1. Start by heating a pot and then add in quinoa. Stir until it cooks and turns a golden color.
2. Add in your peanut butter, melted chocolate, and vanilla before mixing well.
3. Pour this mixture onto a baking sheet, and make sure it's spread out evenly.
4. Place it in the fridge for three to four hours, and break into pieces before serving.

Poached Pears

Serves: 4

Time: 45 Minutes

Calories: 140

Protein: 1 Gram

Fat: 0.5 Grams

Carbs: 34 Grams

Sodium: 9 mg

Ingredients:

- 4 Pears, Whole
- ¼ Cup Apple Juice
- 1 Cup Orange Juice
- 1 Teaspoon Cinnamon
- 1 Teaspoon Nutmeg
- ½ Cup Raspberries, Fresh

- 2 Tablespoons Orange Zest

Directions:

1. Combine your apple juice, orange juice, nutmeg and cinnamon in a bowl.

2. Peel your pears and make sure to leave the stems on.

3. Remove the core, but make sure to remove them from the bottom.

4. Combine your juices and pears in a shallow pan. Cook over medium heat, and bring it to a simmer.

5. Allow it to simmer for a half hour.

6. Turn them regularly, making sure they don't come to a boil.

7. Garnish with orange zest and raspberries.

Marinated Berries

Serves: 2

Time: 2 Hours 5 Minutes

Calories: 176

Protein: 2 Grams

Fat: 4 Grams

Carbs: 33 Grams

Ingredients:

- ¼ Cup Balsamic Vinegar
- ½ Cup Strawberries
- ½ Cup Blueberries
- ½ Cup Raspberries
- 2 Shortbread Biscuits
- 2 Tablespoons Brown Sugar, Packed
- 1 Teaspoon Vanilla Extract, Pure

Directions:

1. Start by mixing your brown sugar, vanilla and balsamic vinegar in a bowl, and then blend your berries in another bowl. Pour your marinate on top of the fruit, and allow it to marinate for ten to fifteen minutes.
2. Drain, and then allow it to chill for up to two hours.
3. Distribute the chilled fruit in bowls served with shortbread on the side.

Baked Apple Delight

Serves: 6

Time: 1 Hour 10 Minutes

Calories: 200

Protein: 2 Grams

Fat: 4 Grams

Carbs: 39 Grams

Sodium: 7 mg

Ingredients:

- 6 Apples
- 3 Tablespoons Almonds, Chopped
- 1/3 Cup Cherries, Dried & Chopped Coarsely
- 1 Tablespoon Wheat Germ
- 1 Tablespoon Brown Sugar
- ¼ Cup Water
- ½ Cup Apple Juice
- 1/8 Teaspoon Nutmeg
- ½ Teaspoon Cinnamon
- 2 Tablespoons Dark Honey, Raw
- 2 Teaspoons Walnut Oil

Directions:

1. Start by heating your oven to 350, and then blend your almonds, wheat germ, brown sugar, cherries, nutmeg and cinnamon in a bowl. Set this bowl to the side.
2. Core your apples starting from their stem, and chop into ¾ inch pieces.
3. Place this mixture into each hole.
4. Arrange the apples upright in a baking dish. A small one will work best. Pour in your apple juice and water, and then drizzle the oil and honey over top.
5. Cover with foil, and cook for fifty to sixty minutes. The apples should be tender.
6. Serve at room temperature or immediately.

Easy Apricot Biscotti

Serves: 24

Time: 1 Hour 10 Minutes

Calories: 75

Protein: 2 Grams

Fat: 2 Grams

Carbs: 12 Grams

Sodium: 17 mg

Ingredients:

- 2 Tablespoon Olive Oil
- ¼ Cup Almonds, Chopped Coarse
- ¾ Cup Whole Wheat Flour
- ½ Teaspoon Almond Extract, Pure
- 2/3 Cup Dried Apricots, Chopped
- 2 Tablespoons Dark Honey, Raw
- 2 Eggs, Lightly Beaten
- 1 Teaspoon Baking Powder
- ¼ Cup Brown Sugar

- 2 Tablespoons Milk, 1%
- ¾ Cup All Purpose Flour

Directions:

1. Preheat your stove to 350, and then get out a bowl. Whisk your all-purpose whole wheat flour and baking powder together.

2. Add in your milk, honey, canola oil, eggs and almond extract together. Stir until it become a dough like consistency and then add in your almonds and apricots.

3. Place flours on your hands and then mix everything together. Place your dough on a cookie sheet and flatten it to be about a foot long and three inches wide. It should be about an inch tall.

4. Bake for twenty-five to thirty minutes. It should be light brown.

5. Take it out and allow it to cool for ten to fifteen minutes. Cut into twenty-four slices by cutting crosswise.

6. Arrange the cut slices face down on the baking sheet, baking for another fifteen to twenty minutes. It should be crisp, and allow it to cool before serving.

Watermelon Bowl

Serves: 32

Time: 1 Hour 10 Minutes

Calories: 111

Protein: 2 Grams

Fat: 0 Grams

Carbs: 26 Grams

Sodium: 7 mg

Ingredients:

- 1 Watermelon, Halved Lengthwise
- 3 Tablespoons Lime Juice, Fresh
- 1 Cup Sugar
- 1 ½ Cup Water
- 1 ½ Cups Mint Leaves, Fresh & Chopped
- 6 Plums, Pitted & Halved
- 1 Cantaloupe, Small

- 4 Nectarines, Pitted & Halved
- 1 lb. Green Grapes, Seedless

Directions:

1. Mix sugar and water in a two-quart pot and bring it to a boil using medium heat. Stir your sugar in until it dissolves.
2. Mix in your lime juice and mint, and then place it in the fridge until chilled.
3. Chop your watermelon and cantaloupe into bite sized pieces, and then slice the nectarines and plums into wedges.
4. Mix all your fruit together in a large bowl before adding in your grapes.
5. Take the mixture out of the fridge and pour it over the fruit.
6. Mix well, and then cover it with saran wrap.
7. Refrigerate for two hours, and stir occasionally. Serve chilled.

Red Egg Skillet

Serves: 6

Time: 15 Minutes

Calories: 188

Protein: 10.3 Grams

Fat: 15.5 Grams

Carbs: 2.6 Grams

Sodium: 160 mg

Ingredients:

- 7 Greek Olives, Pitted & Sliced
- 3 Tomatoes, Ripe & Diced
- 2 Tablespoons Olive oil
- 4 Eggs

- ¼ Cup Parsley, Fresh & Chopped
- 1/8 Teaspoon Sea Salt, Fine
- Black Pepper to Taste

Directions:

1. Get out a pan and grease it. Throw your tomatoes in and cook for ten minutes before adding in your olives. Cook for another five minutes.
2. Add your eggs into the pan, cooking over medium-heat so that your eggs are cooked all the way through.
3. Season with salt and pepper and serve topped with parsley.

Roasted Plum with Almonds

Serves: 6

Time: 45 Minutes

Calories: 204

Protein: 2 Grams

Fat: 9 Grams

Carbs: 31 Grams

Sodium: 64 mg

Ingredients:

- 6 Plums, Large, Pitted & Halved
- 3 Tablespoons butter
- 1/3 Cup Brown Sugar
- 2 Cups Fennel, Sliced
- ¼ Cup All Purpose Flour
- 1/3 Cup Almonds, Sliced

Directions:

1. Heat your oven to 425, and then place the plums in a shallow baking dish.
2. Get out a shallow baking dish and place your plums inside.
3. Get out a bowl and mix your brown sugar and butter together until smooth, and blend in your flour. Make sure it's mixed well, and then toss in your almonds.
4. Pour the mixture over the plums evenly, and then bake for twenty-five to thirty minutes. The plums should be tender.

Cappuccino Muffins

Serves: 12

Time: 25 Minutes

Calories: 495

Protein: 29.3 Grams

Fat: 5.1 Grams

Carbs: 93.2 Grams

Ingredients:

- 2 Cups Flour, All Purpose/1 Egg
- ½ Cup Cream
- 1 Tablespoon Baking Powder
- 1/8 Teaspoon Sea Salt, Fine
- ½ Cup Brown Sugar
- 1 Cup Coffee, Cold
- Powdered Sugar for Garnish

Directions:

1. Start by heating your oven to 350, and then grease a muffin tray using butter.
2. Sift your salt, baking powder and flour together in a bowl.
3. Beat your eggs along with your cream together until it's blended well.
4. Pour this mixture in a floured bowl, and mix well.
5. Stir in your coffee, and then divide between your muffin tins.
6. Bake for twenty minutes, and serve garnished with powder sugar.

Mediterranean Toast

Serves: 1

Time: 10 Minutes

Calories: 314

Protein: 4.2 Grams

Fat: 28.7 Grams

Carbs: 13.2 Grams

Sodium: 84 mg

Ingredients:

- 1 Slice Whole Wheat Bread
- 1 Tablespoon Roasted Red Pepper Hummus
- 3 Cherry Tomatoes, Sliced
- ¼ Avocado, Mashed
- 3 Greek Olives, Sliced
- 1 Hardboiled Egg, Sliced
- 1 ½ Teaspoons Crumbled Feta Cheese, Reduced Fat

Directions:

1. Start by topping your toast with ¼ avocado and then your hummus. Add your remaining ingredients and season with salt and pepper before serving.

Lunch Recipes

Mediterranean Quiche

Serves: 6

Time: 25 Minutes

Calories: 417

Protein: 14.5 Grams

Fat: 13.3 Grams

Carbs: 13.9 Grams

Sodium: 155 mg

Ingredients

- ½ Cup Sundried Tomatoes
- 2 Cloves Garlic, Minced
- 1 Onion, Diced
- 2 Tablespoons Butter
- 1 Prepared Pie Crust
- Boiling Water
- 1 Red Pepper, Diced
- 2 Cups Spinach, Fresh
- ¼ Cup Kalamata Olives
- 1 Teaspoon Oregano

- 1 Teaspoon Parsley
- 1/3 Cup Feta Cheese, Crumbled
- 4 Eggs, Large
- 1 ¼ Cup Milk
- Sea Salt & Black Pepper to Taste
- 1 Cup Cheddar Cheese, Shredded & Divided

Directions:

1. Add your tomatoes to boiling water and allow it to cook for five minutes before draining.

2. Chop the tomatoes before setting them to the side, and adjust the oven to 375.

3. Spread the pie crust into a nine-inch pie pan, and heat the butter and add in your garlic and onion.

4. Cook for three minutes before adding in your red pepper, and then cook for another three minutes.

5. Add in your parsley and oregano before adding in your spinach and olives. Cook for about another five minutes. Take it off heat, and then add in your feta cheese and tomatoes.

6. Spread your mixture into the prepared pie crust, and then beat the egg and milk. Season with salt and pepper and then add in half a cup of cheese.

7. Pour this mixture over your spinach, and then bake for fifty-five minutes. It should be golden, and serve warm.

Grilled Fish with Lemons

Serves: 4

Time: 20 Minutes

Calories: 147

Protein: 22 Grams **Fat:** 1 Gram

Carbs: 4 Grams **Sodium:** 158 mg

Ingredients:

- 3-4 Lemons
- 1 Tablespoon Olive Oil
- Sea Salt & Black Pepper to Taste
- 4 Catfish Fillets, 4 Ounces Each
- Nonstick Cooking Spray

Directions:

1. Pat your fillets dry using a paper towel and let them come to room temperature. This may take ten minutes. Coat the cooking grate of your grill with nonstick cooking spray while it's cold. Once it's coated preheat it to 400 degrees.

2. Cut one lemon in half, setting it to the side. Slice your remaining half of the lemon into ¼ inch slices. Get out a bowl and squeeze a tablespoon of juice from your reserved half. Add your oil to the bowl, mixing well.

3. Brush your fish down with the oil and lemon mixture.

4. Place your lemon slices on the grill and then put our fillets on top. Grill with your lid closed. Turn the fish halfway through if they're more than a half an inch thick.

Pesto Walnut Noodles

Serves: 4

Time: 25 Minutes

Calories: 301

Protein: 7 Grams

Fat: 28 Grams

Carbs: 11 Grams

Sodium: 160 mg

Ingredients:

- 4 Zucchini, Made into Zoodles
- ¼ Cup Olive Oil, Divided
- ½ Teaspoon Crushed Red Pepper
- 2 Cloves Garlic, Minced & Divided
- ¼ Teaspoon Black Pepper
- ¼ Teaspoon sea Salt
- 2 Tablespoons Parmesan Cheese, Grated & Divided
- 1 Cup Basil, Fresh & Packed
- ¾ Cup Walnut Pieces, Divided

Directions:

1. Start by making your zucchini noodles by using a spiralizer to get ribbons. Combine your zoodles with a minced garlic clove and tablespoon of oil. Season with salt and pepper and crushed red pepper. Set it to the side.

2. Get out a large skillet and heat a ½ a tablespoon of oil over medium-high heat. Add in half of your zoodles, cooking for five minutes. You will need to stir every minute or so. Repeat with another ½ a tablespoon of oil and your remaining zoodles.

3. Make your pesto while your zoodles cook. Put your garlic clove, a tablespoon or parmesan, basil leaves and ¼ cup of walnuts in your food processor. Season with salt and pepper if desired, and drizzle the remaining two tablespoons of oil in until completely blended.

4. Add the pesto to your zoodles, topping with remaining walnuts and parmesan to serve.

Tomato Tabbouleh

Serves: 4

Time: 30 Minutes

Calories: 314

Protein: 8 Grams

Fat: 15 Grams

Carbs: 41 Grams

Sodium: 141

Ingredients:

- 8 Beefsteak Tomatoes
- ½ Cup Water
- 3 Tablespoons Olive Oil, Divided
- ½ Cup Whole Wheat Couscous, Uncooked
- 1 ½ Cups Parsley, Fresh & Minced
- 2 Scallions Chopped
- 1/3 Cup Mint, Fresh & Minced
- Sea Salt & Black Pepper to Taste
- 1 Lemon
- 4 Teaspoons Honey, Raw
- 1/3 Cup Almonds, Chopped

Directions:

1. Start by heating your oven to 400 degrees. Take your tomato and slice the top off each one before scooping the flesh out. Put the tops flesh and seeds in a mixing bowl.

2. Get out a baking dish before adding in a tablespoon of oil to grease it. Place your tomatoes in the dish, and then cover your dish with foil.

3. Now you will make your couscous while your tomatoes cook. Bring the water to a boil using a saucepan and then add the couscous in and cover. Remove it form heat, and allow it to sit for five minutes. Fluff it with a fork.

4. Chop your tomato flesh and tops up, and then drain the excess water using a colander. Measure a cup of your chopped tomatoes and place them back in the mixing bowl. Mix with mint scallions, pepper, salt and parsley.

5. Zest your lemon into the bowl, and then half the lemon. Squeeze the lemon juice in, and mix well.

6. Add your tomato mix to the couscous.

7. Carefully remove your tomatoes from the oven and hen divide your tabbouleh among your tomatoes. Cover the pan with foil and then put it in the oven. Cook for another eight to ten minutes. Your tomatoes should be firm but still tender.

8. Drizzle with honey and top with almonds before serving.

Lemon Faro Bowl

Serves: 6

Time: 25 Minutes

Calories: 279

Protein: 7 Grams

Fat: 14 Grams

Carbs: 36 Grams

Sodium: 118 mg

Ingredients:

- 1 Tablespoon + 2 Teaspoons Olive Oil, Divided
- 1 Cup Onion, Chopped
- 2 Cloves Garlic, Minced
- 1 Carrot, Shredded
- 2 Cups Vegetable Broth, Low Sodium
- 1 Cup Pearled Faro
- 2 Avocados, Peeled, Pitted & Sliced

- 1 Lemon, Small

- Sea Salt to Taste

Directions:

1. Start by placing a saucepan over medium-high heat. Add in a tablespoon of oil and then throw in your onion once the oil is hot. Cook for about five minutes, stirring frequently to keep it from burning.

2. Add in your carrot and garlic. Allow it to cook for abut another minute while you continue to stir.

3. Add in your broth and faro. Allow it to come to a boil and adjust your heat to high to help. Once it boils, lower it to medium-low and cover your saucepan. Let it simmer for twenty minutes. The faro should be al dente and plump.

4. Pour the faro into a bowl and add in your avocado and zest. Drizzle with your remaining oil and add in your lemon wedges.

Chickpea & Red Pepper Delight

Serves: 3

Time: 30 Minutes

Calories: 195

Protein: 9.3 Grams

Fat: 8.5 Grams

Carbs: 25.5 Grams

Sodium: 142 mg

Ingredients:

- 1 Red Bell Pepper, Diced
- 2 Cups Water
- 4 Sun-Dried Tomatoes
- ¼ Cup Red Wine Vinegar
- 2 Tablespoon Olive Oil
- 2 Cloves Garlic, Chopped
- 29 Ounces Chickpeas, Canned, Drained & Rinsed

- ½ Cup Parsley, Chopped **/** Sea Salt to Taste

Directions:

1. Get out a baking sheet and put your red bell pepper on it with the skin side up.
2. Bake for eight minutes. Your skin should bubble, and then place it in a bag to seal it.
3. Remove your bell peppers in about ten minutes, and then slice it into thin slices.
4. Get out two cups of water and pour it in a bowl. Microwave for four minutes and add in your sundried tomatoes, letting them sit for ten minutes. Drain them before slicing into thin strips. Mix your red wine vinegar and garlic with your olive oil. Ross your roasted red bell pepper with parsley, sun dried tomatoes, and chickpeas. Season with salt before serving.

Chickpea Salad

Serves: 6

Time: 10 Minutes

Calories: 231

Protein: 12 Grams

Fat: 12 Grams

Carbs: 8 Grams

Sodium: 160 mg

Ingredients:

- 28 Ounces Chickpeas, Drained
- ½ Red Onion, Chopped Fine
- 2 Cucumbers, Chopped Fine
- ¼ Cup Olive Oil
- 2 Lemons, Juiced
- 1 Lemon, Zested
- 1 Tablespoon Tahini

- 3 Cloves Garlic, Minced

- 2 Teaspoons Oregano

- Sea Salt & Black Pepper to taste

Directions:

1. Get out a bowl and combine your cucumbers with your chickpeas and red onion.

2. Get out a small bowl and whisk your lemon juice, olive oil, lemon zest, tahini, garlic, sea salt, oregano and pepper.

3. Toss the dressing with your salad before serving.

Pesto Pasta

Serves: 4

Time: 10 Minutes

Calories: 405

Protein: 13 Grams

Fat: 21 Grams

Carbs: 44 Grams

Sodium: 141 mg

Ingredients:

- 3 Tablespoons Olive Oil
- 3 Cloves Garlic, Minced Fine
- 1/2 Cup Basil Leaves, Fresh
- ¼ Cup Parmesan Cheese Grated
- ¼ Cup Pine Nuts
- 8 Ounces Whole Wheat Pasta

Directions:

1. Start by cooking your pasta per package instructions.
2. In a blender combine all remaining ingredients to make your pesto.
3. Serve with hot pasta.

Eggplant Rolls

Serves: 6

Time: 16 Minutes

Calories: 91

Protein: 2.1 Grams

Fat: 7 Grams

Carbs: 6.3 Grams

Sodium: 140 mg

Ingredients:

- 1 Eggplant, ½ Inch Sliced Lengthwise
- Sea Salt & black Pepper to Taste
- 1 Tablespoon Olive Oil
- 1/3 Cup Cream Cheese
- ½ Cup Tomatoes, Chopped
- 1 Clove Garlic, Minced
- 2 Tablespoons Dill, Chopped

Directions:

1. Slice your eggplant before brushing it down with olive oil. Season your eggplant slices with salt and pepper.

2. Grill the eggplants for three minutes per side.

3. Get out a bowl and combine cream cheese, garlic, dill and tomatoes in a different bowl.

4. Allow your eggplant slices to cool and then spread the mixture over each one. Roll them and pin them with a toothpick to serve.

Heavenly Quinoa

Serves: 5

Time: 20 Minutes

Calories: 344

Protein: 12.6 Grams

Fat: 13.8 Grams

Carbs: 45.7 Grams

Sodium: 96 mg

Ingredients:

- 1 Cup Almonds
- 1 Cup Quinoa
- 1 Teaspoon Cinnamon
- 1 Pinch Sea Salt
- 1 Teaspoon Vanilla Extract, Pure
- 2 Cups Milk
- 2 Tablespoons Honey, Raw
- 3 Dates, Dried, Pitted & Chopped Fine
- 5 Apricots, Dried & Chopped Fine

Directions:

1. Get out a skillet to toast your almonds in for about five minutes. The should be golden and aromatic.

2. Place your quinoa and cinnamon in a saucepan using medium heat. Add in your vanilla, salt and milk. Stir and then bring it to a boil. Reduce your heat, and allow it to simmer for fifteen minutes.

3. Add in your dates, honey, apricots and half of your almonds.

4. Serve topped with almonds and parsley if desired.

Red Bean & Green Salad

Serves: 6

Time: 10 Minutes **Calories:** 242

Protein: 10.1 Grams **Fat:** 13.7 Grams

Carbs: 22.7 Grams **Sodium:** 121 mg

Ingredients:

- 1 Cup Red Beans, Cooked & Drained
- 1 Cup Lettuce, Shredded & Chopped
- 2 Cups Spinach Leaves
- 1 Cup Red Onions, Sliced into Thin Rings
- ½ Cup Walnuts, Halved
- 3 Tablespoon Olive Oil
- 3 Tablespoons Lemon Juice, Fresh
- 1 Clove Garlic, Minced
- 1 Teaspoon Dijon Mustard
- ¼ Teaspoon Sea Salt, Fine **/** ¼ Teaspoon Black Pepper

Directions:

1. Combine your lettuce, spinach, walnut, red beans and red onion together.
2. In a different bowl mix your olive oil, garlic, Dijon mustard and lemon juice together to form your dressing.
3. Drizzle the dressing over the salad and adjust salt and pepper as necessary.
4. Serve immediately.

Dinner Recipes

Vegetable Stew

Serves: 6

Time: 45 Minutes

Calories: 179

Protein: 4 Grams

Fat: 5.3 Grams

Carbs: 31.4 Grams

Sodium: 130 mg

Ingredients:

- 2 Tablespoons Olive Oil
- 2 Onions, Chopped Fine
- 1 Clove Garlic, Chopped Fine
- 2 Bell Peppers, Chopped
- 4 Tomatoes, Diced
- 2 Carrots, Large & Chopped
- ½ Cup Green Beans, Chopped
- 2 Teaspoons Cumin
- 1 Cup Water
- 1 Teaspoon Red Hot Pepper Flakes
- ½ Teaspoon Turmeric

- Sea Salt & Black Pepper to Taste
- 2 Teaspoon Coriander Leaves, Fresh & Chopped to Garnish

Directions:

1. Get out a pan and place your oil in it. Sauté over medium-heat, cooking your onions and garlic. Your onions should turn golden brown.
2. Add in your tomatoes, peppers, and carrots. Cook for five minutes.
3. Add in your green beans and potatoes, sautéing for another five minutes.
4. Pour in your water and bring it to a boil. Allow it to simmer for twenty minutes. Your vegetables should be tender when you're done.
5. Season with turmeric, red pepper flakes, cumin, salt and pepper.
6. Garnish with coriander before serving.

Easy Greek Soup

Serves: 4

Time: 35 Minutes

Calories: 568

Protein: 24 Grams

Fat: 20.7 Grams

Carbs: 66 Grams

Sodium: 98 mg

Ingredients:

- 1 Cup Asparagus, Chopped
- 1 Egg, Large
- ½ Lemon, Juiced
- 6 Cups Chicken Broth
- 1 ½ Cups Chicken, Shredded & Cooked
- 2 Tablespoons Olive Oil
- 1 Onion, Small & Diced
- 1/3 Cup Arborio Rice
- ½ Cup Dill, Fresh, Chopped & Divided
- 1 Cup Carrots, Diced
- Sea Salt & Black Pepper to Taste
- Chives, Fresh & Minced for Garnish

Directions:

1. Add in your onions with two tablespoons of oil to a pan and cook for five minutes.

2. Add in ¼ cup of dill with a bay leaf and add in chicken broth. Allow it to cook for ten minutes.

3. Stir in the carrots and asparagus and allow it to cook for fifteen minutes. Add the chicken and allow it to simmer using low heat, and then beat your eggs with two tablespoons of water. Add in your lemon juice, making sure it's mixed well.

4. Pour this into your cooking soup.

5. Cook until it thickens, and then add your dill, salt and pepper. Serve warm.

Seafood Gumbo

Serves: 5

Time: 40 Minutes

Calories: 385

Protein: 38.2 Grams

Fat: 16.5 Grams

Carbs: 19.4 Grams

Sodium: 116 mg

Ingredients:

- ¼ Cup Olive Oil
- ¼ Cup Flour, Gluten Free
- 1 White Onion, Chopped
- 1 Cup Celery, Chopped
- 1 Red + Green Bell Pepper, Chopped

- 1 Red Chili, Chopped
- 1 Cup Crushed Tomatoes, Canned
- 2 Cloves Garlic, Crushed
- 1 Bay Leaf
- 16 Ounces Crab Meat, Canned
- 2 Cups Okra, Chopped
- 1 Teaspoon Thyme, Dried
- 2 Cups Fish Stock
- 1 Teaspoon Cayenne Powder
- 1 lb. Shrimp, Peeled & Deveined
- Sea Salt & Black Pepper to Taste
- ¼ Cup Parsley, Fresh & Chopped Fine

Directions:

1. Get out an eight-quart pot and heat your oil in it. Add in your flour once your oil is hot, and stir to cook for five minutes.
2. Stir in your okra, onion and peppers. Cook for another five minutes before adding in your stock, garlic, thyme, tomatoes and bay leaf. Mix well, and then allow your mixture to come to a boil.
3. Decrease your heat to let it simmer for fifteen minutes.
4. Add in your shrimp and crabmeat, cooking for eight minutes and then add in your parsley.
5. Serve topped with green onions while warm.

Roasted Squash Bisque

Serves: 2

Time: 1 Hour 15 Minutes **Calories:** 244

Protein: 6 Grams **Fat:** 13 Grams

Carbs: 32 Grams **Sodium:** 90 mg

Ingredients:

- 1 ½ Cups Winter Squash, Chopped
- 1 Clove Garlic, Minced
- Sea Salt & Black Pepper to Taste
- 1 Cup Vegetable Broth, Low Sodium
- ¼ Teaspoon Nutmeg
- 1/3 Cup Almond Milk, Unsweetened **/** ¼ Cup Pistachios, Chopped Fine

Directions:

1. Start by heating your oven to 375, and then spread your squash on a baking sheet. Bake for forty minutes to one hours. The flesh should be tender. Allow your squash to cool, and then place it in a food processor.

2. Add in your pepper, garlic, nutmeg and broth. Blend until smooth.

3. Pour this soup mixture into a large saucepan and place it over a low heat. Stir constantly until your soup comes to a boil, which should take about five minutes.

4. Stir in your almond milk, and allow it to continue to cook and bubble for about five minutes.

5. Garnish with chopped pistachios before serving.

Chickpea Patties

Serves: 8

Time: 25 Minutes

Calories: 352

Protein: 6.1 Grams

Fat: 27.1 Grams

Carbs: 24 Grams

Sodium: 160 mg

Ingredients:

- 1 Cup Flour
- ¾ Cup Hot Water
- 1 Egg, Whisked
- ½ Teaspoon Cumin
- ½ Teaspoon Sea Salt, Fine
- 1 Cup Spinach, Fresh & Chopped
- 3 Cloves Garlic, Minced
- 1/8 Teaspoon Baking Soda

- ¾ Cup Chickpeas, Cooked
- 2 Scallions, Small & Chopped
- 1 Cup Olive Oil

Directions:

1. Get out a bowl and mix your salt, cumin and flour together. Add in your water and egg to form a batter. Whisk well. It should thicken.

2. Stir in your baking soda, garlic, spinach, chickpeas, and scallions, blending well.

3. Get a pan and place it over high heat. Add in your oil. Once your oil begins o simmer pour in t tablespoon of your batter, frying on both sides. Repeat until all your batter is used.

4. Garnish with lime and greens before serving.

Red Onion Tilapia

Serves: 4

Time: 15 Minutes

Calories: 200

Protein: 22 Grams

Fat: 11 Grams

Carbs: 4 Grams

Sodium: 151

Ingredients:

- 1 Tablespoon Olive Oil
- 1 Tablespoon Orange Juice, Fresh
- ¼ Teaspoon Sea Salt, Fine
- 1 Avocado, Pitted, Skinned & Sliced
- ¼ Cup Red Onion, Chopped
- 4 Tilapia Fillets, 4 Ounces Each

Directions:

1. Start by getting out a pie dish that is nine inches. Glass is best. Use a fork to mix your slat, orange juice and oil together. Dip one filet at a time and then put them in your dish. They should be coated on both sides. Put them in a wheel formation so that each fillet is in the center of the dish and draped over the edge. Top each fillet with a tablespoon of onion. Fold the fillet that's hanging over your pie dish in half so that it's over the onion.

2. Cover it with plastic wrap but don't close it all the way. They should be able to vent the steam. Microwave for three minutes.

3. Tip with avocado to serve.

Chicken & Asparagus

Serves: 4

Time: 20 Minutes

Calories: 530

Protein: 36.8 Grams

Fat: 33.3 Grams

Carbs: 28.8 Grams

Sodium: 130 mg

Ingredients:

- 1 lb. Chicken Breast, Boneless & Skinless
- ¼ Cup Flour
- 4 Tablespoons Butter
- ½ Teaspoon Sea Salt, Fine
- ½ Teaspoon Black Pepper
- 1 Teaspoon Lemon Pepper Seasoning
- 2 Slices Lemon
- 1-2 Cups Asparagus, Chopped

- 2 Tablespoons Honey, Raw
- Parsley to Garnish

Directions:

1. Cover your chicken using plastic wrap and beat it until it's ¾ of an inch thick.

2. Get out a bowl and mix your slat, flour and pepper together. Coat your chicken in your flour mixture.

3. Get out a pan to melt two tablespoons of butter over medium-high heat.

4. Place the chicken breast in the pan to cook for three to five minutes. It should turn golden brown on each side.

5. While your chicken is cooking sprinkle the lemon on each side. Once it's cooked, transfer it to a plate. In the same pan add in your asparagus, cooking until it's crisp but tender. It should turn a bright green. Set it to the side.

6. You'll use the same pan to add your lemon slices to caramelize.

Easy Stuffed Peppers

Serves: 6

Time: 1 Hour 10 Minutes **Calories:** 509

Protein: 23.8 Grams **Fat:** 22.8 Grams

Carbs: 45.5 Grams **Sodium:** 20 mg

Ingredients:

- 1 Yellow Onion, Small & Chopped
- 6 Bell Peppers, Cored
- ½ lb. Ground Beef
- 1 Tablespoon Olive Oil
- Sea Salt & Black Pepper to Taste
- ½ Teaspoon Allspice
- ½ Teaspoon Garlic Powder
- 1 Cup Chickpeas, Cooked
- ½ Cup Parsley, Chopped
- 1 Cup Short Grain Rice Soaked in Water for 10-15 Minutes & Drained
- ½ Teaspoon Sweet Paprika

- 1 ¼ Cups Water
- 3 Tablespoons Tomato Sauce
- ¾ Cup Chicken Broth

Directions:

1. Heat your oil over a medium-size pot and sauté your onions until they turn golden and tender.

2. Add in your meat and cook over medium-high temperature and stir well. Stir occasionally so that the meat doesn't clump together, and brown it. Season your ground meat with allspice, garlic powder, salt and pepper. Add in your chickpeas, cooking for a few more minutes.

3. Stir in your rice, paprika, parsley and tomato sauce.

4. Add water and then bring the mixture to a boil. Let it boil until it's been reduced by half. Once it's reduced then lower your heat.

5. Seal your pot an allow it to cook for twenty minutes. Your rice should be fully cooked.

6. Grill your bell pepper using medium-high heat, which should take ten to fifteen minutes. You should do this while your rice cooks, and then make sure to turn the peppers occasionally. All sides should be cooked, and then remove them. Allow them to cool.

7. Heat your oven to 350, and then assemble your peppers by spooning the rice mixture into a baking dish and fill it wit broth. Cover it with foil and then place it in the oven. Cook for about thirty minutes, and garnish with parsley before serving warm.

Beef Kofta

Serves: 4

Time: 30 Minutes

Calories: 216

Protein: 26.1 Grams

Fat: 12.2 Grams

Carbs: 1.3 Grams

Sodium: 152 mg

Ingredients:

- 1 lb. Ground Beef, 93% Lean or More
- ½ Cup Onions, Minced
- 1 Tablespoon Olive Oil
- ½ Teaspoon Sea Salt, Fine
- ½ Teaspoon Coriander, Ground
- ½ Teaspoon Cumin, Ground
- ¼ Teaspoon Cinnamon
- ¼ Teaspoon Mint Leaves, Dried

- ¼ Teaspoon Allspice

Directions:

1. Mix your beef, salt, cumin, coriander, cinnamon, oil, onion, mint and allspice together in a large bowl.
2. Get out wooden skewers and shape beef kebabs from the mixture.
3. Refrigerate for ten minutes before grilling them. You will need to preheat your grill and cook them for fourteen minutes. Remember to turn them constantly to avoid burning.
4. Serve warm.

Herby Chicken with Potatoes

Serves: 6 **Time:** 1 Hour 5 Minutes

Calories: 378 **Protein:** 54.7 Grams

Fat: 16 Grams **Carbs:** 0.7 Grams

Fat: 16 Grams **Sodium:** 69 mg

Ingredients:

- 4 Chicken Thighs, Skin On & Bone In
- 3 Tablespoons Olive Oil, Divided
- ¼ Cup Lemon Juice, Fresh
- 1 Tablespoon Red Wine Vinegar
- 4 Cloves Garlic, Large & Crushed
- 3 Teaspoons Basil
- 2 Teaspoons Parsley
- 2 Teaspoons oregano
- 2 Teaspoons Sea Salt, Fine
- 8 Baby Potatoes, Halved
- 1 Red Onion, Cut into Wedges
- 1 Red Bell Pepper, Cut into Wedges
- 4 Tablespoons Kalamata Olives, Pitted
- 1 Zucchini, Sliced
- Lemon Slices to Serve

Directions:

1. Mix your vinegar, garlic, basil, parsley, oregano, salt, and vinegar together with two tablespoons of olive oil.

2. Pour half of the mixture into your chicken, rubbing it down so that it's coated well.

3. Cover your chicken and allow it to marinate for fifteen minutes.

4. Heat your oven to 430, and then get out a skillet.

5. Place a tablespoon of olive into your skillet, and sear the chicken for four minutes per side.

6. Add your vegetables, and then pour in your reserved marinade, making sure it's mixed well before covering your skillet.

7. Bake for thirty-five minutes before taking the lid off.

8. Broil for five minutes in the oven before serving warm with lemon and olives on top.

Side Dish Recipes

Pistachio Arugula Salad

Serves: 6

Time: 20 Minutes **Calories:** 150

Protein: 5 Grams **Fat:** 12 Grams

Carbs: 8 Grams **Sodium:** 169 mg

Ingredients:

- ¼ Cup Olive Oil
- 6 Cups Kale, Chopped Rough
- 2 Cups arugula
- ½ Teaspoon Smoked Paprika
- 2 Tablespoons Lemon Juice, Fresh
- 1/3 Cup Pistachios, Unsalted & Shelled
- 6 Tablespoons Parmesan, Grated

Directions:

1. Get out a large bowl and combine your oil, lemon juice, kale and smoked paprika. Massage it into the leaves for about fifteen seconds. You then need to allow it to sit for ten minutes.

2. Mix everything together before serving with grated cheese on top.

Potato Salad

Serves: 6

Time: 20 Minutes

Calories: 175

Protein: 3 Grams

Fat: 7 Grams

Carbs: 27 Grams

Sodium: 98 mg

Ingredients:

- 2 lbs. Golden Potatoes, Cubed in 1 Inch Pieces
- 3 Tablespoons Olive Oil
- 3 tablespoons Lemon Juice, Fresh
- 1 Tablespoon Olive Brine
- ¼ Teaspoon Sea Salt, Fine
- ½ Cup Olives, Sliced
- 1 Cup Celery, Sliced
- 2 Tablespoons Oregano, Fresh

- 2 Tablespoons Mint Leaves, Fresh & Chopped

Directions:

1. Get out a medium saucepan and put your potatoes in cold water. The water should b earn inch above your potatoes. Set it over high heat and bring it to a boil before turning the heat down. You want to turn it down to medium-low. Allow it to cook for twelve to fifteen more minutes. The potatoes should be tender when you pierce them with a fork.

2. Get out a small bowl and whisk your oil, lemon juice, olive brine and salt together.

3. Drain your potatoes using a colander and transfer it to a serving bowl. Pour in three tablespoons of dressing over your potatoes, and mix well with oregano, and min along with the remaining dressing.

Raisin Rice Pilaf

Serves: 5

Time: 15 Minutes **Calories:** 320

Protein: 6 Grams **Fat:** 7 Grams

Carbs: 61 Grams **Sodium:** 37 mg

Ingredients:

- 1 Tablespoon Olive Oil
- 1 Teaspoon Cumin
- 1 Cup Onion, Chopped
- ½ Cup Carrot, Shredded
- ½ Teaspoon Cinnamon
- 2 Cups Instant Brown Rice / 1 ¾ Cup Orange Juice
- 1 Cup Golden Raisins / ¼ Cup Water
- ½ Cup Pistachios, Shelled / Fresh Chives, Chopped for Garnish

Directions:

1. Place a medium saucepan over medium-high heat before adding in your oil. Add n your onion, and stir often so it doesn't burn. Cook for about five minutes and then add in your cumin, cinnamon and carrot. Cook for about another minute.

2. Add in your orange juice, water and rice. Bring it all to a boil before covering your saucepan. Turn the heat down to medium-low and then allow it to simmer for six to seven minutes. Your rice should be cooked all the way through, and all the liquid should be absorbed.

3. Stir in your pistachios, chives and raisins. Serve warm.

Lebanesen Delight

Serves: 5

Time: 25 Minutes

Calories: 259

Protein: 7 Grams

Fat: 4 Grams

Carbs: 49 Grams

Sodium: 123 mg

Ingredients:

- 1 Tablespoon Olive Oil
- 1 Cup Vermicelli (Can be Substituted for Thin Spaghetti) Broken into 1 to 1 ½ inch Pieces
- 3 Cups Cabbage, Shredded
- 3 Cups Vegetable Broth, Low Sodium
- ½ Cup Water
- 1 Cup Instant Brown Rice
- ¼ Teaspoon Sea Salt, Fine
- 2 Cloves Garlic
- ¼ Teaspoon Crushed Red Pepper
- ½ Cup Cilantro Fresh & Chopped
- Lemon Slices to Garnish

Directions:

1. Get out a saucepan and then place it over medium-high heat. Add in your oil and once it's hot you will need to add in your pasta. Cook for three minutes or until your pasta is toasted. You will have to stir often in order to keep it from burning.

2. Ad in your cabbage, cooking for another four minutes. Continue to stir often.

3. Add in your water and rice. Season with salt, red pepper and garlic before bringing it all to a boil over high heat. Stir, and then cover. Once it's covered turn the heat down to medium-low. Allow it all to simmer for ten minutes.

4. Remove the pan from the burner and then allow it to sit without lifting the lid for five minutes. Take the garlic cloves out and then mash them using a fork. Place them back in, and stir them into the rice. Stir in your cilantro as well and serve warm. Garnish with lemon wedges if desired.

Mediterranean Sweet Potato

Serves: 4

Time: 25 Minutes

Calories: 313

Protein: 8.6 Grams

Carbs: 55 Grams

Sodium: 82 mg

Ingredients:

- 4 Sweet Potatoes
- 15 Ounce Can Chickpeas, Rinsed & Drained
- ½ Tablespoon Olive Oil
- ½ Teaspoon Cumin
- ½ Teaspoon Coriander
- ½ Teaspoon Cinnamon
- 1 Pinch Sea Salt, Fine
- ½ Teaspoon Paprika
- ¼ Cup Hummus
- 1 Tablespoon Lemon Juice, Fresh
- 2-3 Teaspoon Dill, Fresh
- 3 Cloves Garlic, Minced
- Unsweetened Almond Milk as Needed

Directions:

1. Start by preheating your oven to 400, and then get out a baking sheet. Line it with foil.

2. Wash your sweet potatoes before halving them lengthwise.

3. Take your olive oil, cumin, chickpeas, coriander, sea salt and paprika on your baking sheet. Rub the sweet potatoes with olive oil, placing them face down over the mixture.

4. Roast for twenty to twenty-five minutes. They should become tender, and your chickpeas should turn a golden color.

5. Once it's in the oven, you can prepare your sauce. To do this mix your dill, lemon juice, hummus, garlic and a dah of almond milk. Mix well. Add more almond milk to thin as necessary. Adjust the seasoning if necessary.

6. Smash the insides of the sweet potato down, topping with chickpea mixture and sauce before serving.

Flavorful Braised Kale

Serves: 6

Time: 30 Minutes

Calories: 70

Protein: 4 Grams

Fat: 0.5 Grams

Carbs: 9 Grams

Sodium: 133 mg

Ingredients:

- 1 lb. Kale, Stems Removed & Chopped Roughly
- 1 Cup Cherry Tomatoes, Halved
- 2 Teaspoons Olive Oil
- 4 Cloves Garlic, Sliced Thin
- ½ Cup Vegetable Stock
- ¼ Teaspoon Sea Salt, Fine
- 1 Tablespoon Lemon Juice, Fresh
- 1/8 Teaspoon Black Pepper

Directions:

1. Start by heating your olive oil in a frying pan using medium heat, and add in your garlic. Sauté for a minute or two until lightly golden.

2. Mix your kale and vegetable stock with your garlic, adding it to your pan.

3. Cover the pan and then turn the heat down to medium-low.

4. Allow it to cook until your kale wilts and part of your vegetable stock should be dissolved. It should take roughly five minutes.

5. Stir in your tomatoes and cook without a lid until your kale is tender, and then remove it from heat.

6. Mix in your salt, pepper and lemon juice before serving warm.

Bean Salad

Serves: 6

Time: 15 Minutes

Calories: 218

Protein: 7 Grams

Fat: 0 Grams

Carbs: 25 Grams

Sodium: 160 mg

Ingredients:

- 1 Can Garbanzo Beans, Rinsed & Drained
- 2 Tablespoons Balsamic Vinegar
- ¼ Cup Olive Oil
- 4 Cloves Garlic, Chopped Fine
- 1/3 Cup Parsley, Fresh & Chopped
- ¼ Cup Olive Oil
- 1 Red Onion, Diced

- 6 Lettuce Leaves
- ½ Cup Celery, Chopped Fine**/**Black Pepper to Taste

Directions:

1. Make the vinaigrette dressing by whipping together your garlic, parsley, vinegar and pepper in a bowl.

2. Add the olive oil to this mixture and whisk before setting it aside.

3. Add in your onion and beans, and then pour your dressing on top. Toss until it's coated together and then cover it. Place it in the fridge until it's time to serve.

4. Place a lettuce leaf on the plate when serving and spoon the mixture in. garnish with celery.

Basil Tomato Skewers

Serves: 2

Time: 5 Minutes **Calories:** 46

Protein: 7.6 Grams **Fat:** 0.9 Grams

Carbs: 7.3 Grams **Sodium:** 32 mg

Ingredients:

- 16 Mozzarella Balls, Fresh & Small
- 16 Basil Leaves, Fresh
- 16 Cherry Tomatoes
- Olive Oil to Drizzle
- Sea Salt & Black Pepper to Taste

Directions:

1. Start by threading your basil, cheese and tomatoes together on small skewers.
2. Drizzle with oil before seasoning with salt and pepper. Serve immediately.

Olives with Feta

Serves: 4

Time: 5 Minutes

Calories: 71

Protein: 4 Grams

Fat: 2.6 Grams

Carbs: 2 Grams

Sodium: 45 mg

Ingredients:

- ½ Cup Feta Cheese, Diced
- 1 Cup Kalamata Olives, Sliced & Pitted
- 2 Cloves Garlic, Sliced
- 2 Tablespoons Olive Oil
- 1 Lemon, Zested & Juiced
- 1 Teaspoon Rosemary, Fresh & Chopped
- Crushed Red Pepper
- Black Pepper to Taste

Directions:

1. Mix everything together and serve over crackers.

Black Bean Medley

Serves: 4

Time: 5 Minutes **Calories:** 121

Protein: 6 Grams **Fat:** 5 Grams

Carbs: 15 Grams **Sodium:** 17 mg

Ingredients:

- 4 Plum Tomatoes, Chopped

- 14.5 Ounces Black Beans, Canned & Drained

- ½ Red Onion, Sliced

- ¼ Cup Dill, Fresh & Chopped

- 1 Lemon, Juiced

- 2 Tablespoons Olive Oil

- ¼ Cup Feta Cheese, Crumbled

- Sea Salt to Taste

Directions:

1. Mix everything in a bowl except for your feta and salt. Top the beans with salt and feta.

Dessert Recipes

Honey Almonds

Serves: 5

Time: 10 Minutes **Calories:** 149

Protein: 5 Grams **Fat:** 12 Grams

Carbs: 8 Grams **Sodium:** 78 mg

Ingredients:

- 1 Tablespoon Rosemary, Fresh & Minced
- 1 Cup Almonds, Raw & Whole
- 1 Tablespoon Honey, Raw
- ¼ Teaspoon Sea Salt, Fine
- Nonstick Cooking Spray

Directions:

1. Get out a skillet and heat it up over medium heat. In this skillet you'll combine your salt, almonds and rosemary. Mix well. You'll need to cook for a full minute and stir frequently.

2. Drizzle your honey in and cook for another four minutes while stirring frequently. Your almonds should start to darken near the edges and be well coated.

3. Remove your almonds from heat, and spread them onto a pan that's been coated with nonstick cooking spray. They should cool for ten minutes, and then you can break them apart before serving.

Vermicelli Pudding

Serves: 2

Time: 55 Minutes **Calories:** 251

Protein: 11.6 Grams **Fat:** 7.1 Grams

Carbs: 35.7 Grams **Sodium:** 120 mg

Ingredients:

- ½ Cup Vermicelli Noodles
- ½ Cup Sultas
- ½ Teaspoon Vanilla Extract, Pure
- ½ Teaspoon Nutmeg
- 1 Cup Milk
- 2 Tablespoons Sugar
- 2 Eggs

Directions:

1. Start by cooking your vermicelli noodles as your package dictates, and makes sure to drain them.
2. Whisk your eggs, milk and sugar in a bowl.
3. Add in your remaining ingredients.
4. Get out a baking dish and grease it. Place the mixture inside, and then bake at 320 for forty-five minutes.
5. Sprinkle with nutmeg before serving.

Nutty Honey Baked Pears

Serves: 6

Time: 35 Minutes **Calories:** 146

Protein: 3.2 Grams **Fat:** 6.2 Grams

Carbs: 22.1 Grams **Sodium:** 15 mg

Ingredients:

- 3 Pears, Peeled, Halved & Cored
- 1 Teaspoon Butter
- 2 Tablespoons Honey, Raw
- ¼ Cup Pear Nectar
- 1 Tablespoon Orange Zest
- ½ Cup Mascarpone Cheese
- 2 Teaspoons Powdered Sugar
- 1/3 Cup Walnuts

Directions:

1. get out a small bowl and mix your butter honey and pear nectar.
2. Get out a baking dish and then put your pears in, pouring the honey mix over each one.
3. Turn your oven to 350, and then bake for ten minutes.
4. Get out another bowl and combine your mascarpone, orange zest walnuts and powdered sugar.
5. Stuff your pears with the cheese mix and bake for fifteen minutes more.

Glazed Apples

Serves: 4

Time: 15 Minutes

Calories: 264

Protein: 1.8 Grams

Fat: 2.8 Grams

Carbs: 63.7 Grams

Sodium: 3 mg

Ingredients:

- 4 Apples
- ½ Cup Sugar
- ¼ Cup Water
- ½ Cup Orange Juice
- 1 Tablespoon Honey
- 2 Tablespoons Walnuts, Crushed

Directions:

1. Start by getting a pan and placing it over low heat. Caramelize your sugar in water and then add in your honey and orange juice. Bring the mixture to a boil. Allow it to simmer for about two minutes more. It should thicken, but you'll need to stir it constantly.

2. Dip your apple into the Carmel mixture, and then stab it in the middle with a stick.

3. Sprinkle your glazed apples with your crushed walnuts. Serve once hardened.

Dark Chocolate Strawberries

Serves: 8

Time: 25 Minutes **Calories:** 164

Protein: 2.4 Grams **Fat:** 8.3 Grams

Carbs: 21.2 Grams **Sodium:** 18 mg

Ingredients:

- 2 lbs. Strawberries with Stalks

- 1 Cup Dark Chocolate

- 1 Tablespoon Olive Oil

Directions:

1. Start by getting out a double boiling pan and then melt your chocolate in it. Stir in your olive oil before allowing it to cool down

2. Dip each strawberry in by the stalk, making sure each side is coated. Transfer it to a parchment paper, and allow it to cool in your fridge before serving.

Chocolate Fruit Kebabs

Serves: 6

Time: 30 Minutes

Calories: 254

Protein: 3 grams

Fat: 15 Grams

Carbs: 29 Grams

Sodium: 5 mg

Ingredients:

- 8 Ounces Dark Chocolate
- 24 Blueberries, Fresh
- 24 Red Grapes, Seedless
- 12 Cherries, Pitted
- 12 Strawberries, Hulled

Directions:

1. Line a baking sheet with parchment paper. Get out twelve-inch wooden skewers, and then thread your fruit on.

2. Get out a microwave safe bowl, and heat your chocolate for one minute. Stir until all your chocolate is melted.

3. Spon the melted chocolate into a plastic bag, and hen twist it closed. Snip a corner, and then drizzle your chocolate over your fruit kebabs.

4. Allow them to chill in the freezer for twenty minutes before serving.

Vanilla Yogurt Affogato

Serves: 4

Time: 10 Minutes

Calories: 270

Protein: 11 Grams

Fat: 10 Grams

Carbs: 37 Grams

Sodium: 119 mg

Ingredients:

- 2 Teaspoons Sugar
- 4 Shots Hot Espresso
- 24 Ounces Greek Yogurt, Vanilla
- 4 Tablespoon Pistachios, Chopped & Unsalted
- 4 Tablespoons Dark Chocolate Chips

Directions:

1. Spoon your yogurt into four different tall glasses.
2. Mix in a half a teaspoon of sugar into each of your espresso shots. Pour one shot into each yogurt bowl.
3. Top with pistachios and chocolate chips before serving.

Stone Fruit with Whipped Ricotta

Serves: 4

Time: 20 Minutes

Calories: 176

Protein: 7 Grams

Fat: 9 Grams

Carbs: 20 Grams

Sodium: 40 mg

Ingredients:

- 4 Peaches, Halved & Pitted
- Nonstick Cooking Spray
- 2 Teaspoons Olive Oil
- 1 Tablespoon Honey, Raw
- 2 Teaspoons Olive Oil
- ¾ Cup Ricotta Cheese, Whole Milk

- ¼ Teaspoon Nutmeg
- 4 Sprigs Mint for Garnish

Directions:

1. Spray your grill down with the cooking spray while it's cold, and then heat your grill.

2. Take an empty bowl and chill it in the fridge.

3. Take your peaches and brush them all over with oil, and place them cut side down on your grill. Grill for three to five minutes. Grill marks should appear. Turn them over and grill for another four to six minutes. They should be tender.

4. Take the bowl from the fridge and place your ricotta in it. Get out an electric beater and beat it on high speed for two minutes before adding in your nutmeg and add in your honey. Beat for a minute more. Divide the fruit among bowls and top with your ricotta and mint.

Yogurt Cake with Figs

Serves: 6

Time: 1 Hour **Calories:** 290

Protein: 5.9 Grams **Fat:** 14.8 Grams

Carbs: 38.5 Grams **Sodium:** 124 mg

Ingredients:

- 3 Tablespoons All Purpose Flour, Sifted
- ½ Cup Cane Sugar **/** 4 Eggs, Large & Separate
- 1 ½ Cups Greek Yogurt, Full Fat
- ½ Lemon, Juiced & Grated
- 1 ½ Teaspoons Orange Blossom Water (Can be Substituted with Orange Zest & Water)
- Butter for Greasing
- 6 Figs, Fresh & Halved **/** Icing Sugar for Dusting

Directions:

1. Start by heating your oven to 375 and then get out a bowl. Beat your egg yolk with sugar until creamy in a large bowl. Stir in your yogurt, lemon juice, lemon zest, flour, and orange blossom water.
2. Beat your egg white with an electric mixer until it turns foamy, and fold the flour batter and mix gently together until well combined.
3. Get out a nine-inch springform pan, and butter it before pouring your batter in.
4. Bake for fifty minutes, and slice to serve.

Conclusion

Now you know everything you need to in order to get started with the Mediterranean diet, which works best when it's used as a lifestyle choice. Remember that this diet is not meant to limit yourself. Luckily, with the twenty-one day meal plan, you'll be able to get started with simple, easy recipes with easy to find ingredients. Enjoy breakfast to dessert every single day and still reach your health goals.

Made in the USA
Lexington, KY
16 April 2019